# Grandma's Jar of Recipes

MRINAL KARNAD

ISBN
Paperback 979-8-89610-662-3
Hardcase 979-8-89673-468-0

# Author's Note

## Q. Who am I?

Hello to all my readers. I am sure a few of you might not know me, so let me go ahead and introduce myself. I am Mrinal Karnad; a 16 year old teen who likes reading books. Reading being one of my hobbies, I also truly enjoyed the process of writing a book for the first time. In present time, I have read very few books and surely look forward to indulging myself into as many books as I can in the near future

## Q. Why am I writing this, and what made me write a 'BOOK'?

I really don't have a clear explanation for why I'm writing a book, but I will say that there is an author who has truly inspired me when it comes to 'writing' this book and she is Ms. Sudha Murty. The first time I ever

read her book, I remember finishing that 200/300-page book within just 4 days. I really love the way she writes those books and makes the reader a part of the stories. I too have tried my best to write a story that is engaging and one that you will like.

## *Q. So what exactly is this story about?*

This is a story that takes you through the journey of a little girl named Krishna. Krishna too is a teen just like me but she has her own a really wonderful and unusual and a special hobby. This journey also shows you the different shades of a family and how every individual is different, in their own style.

# THE NAIK FAMILY TREE

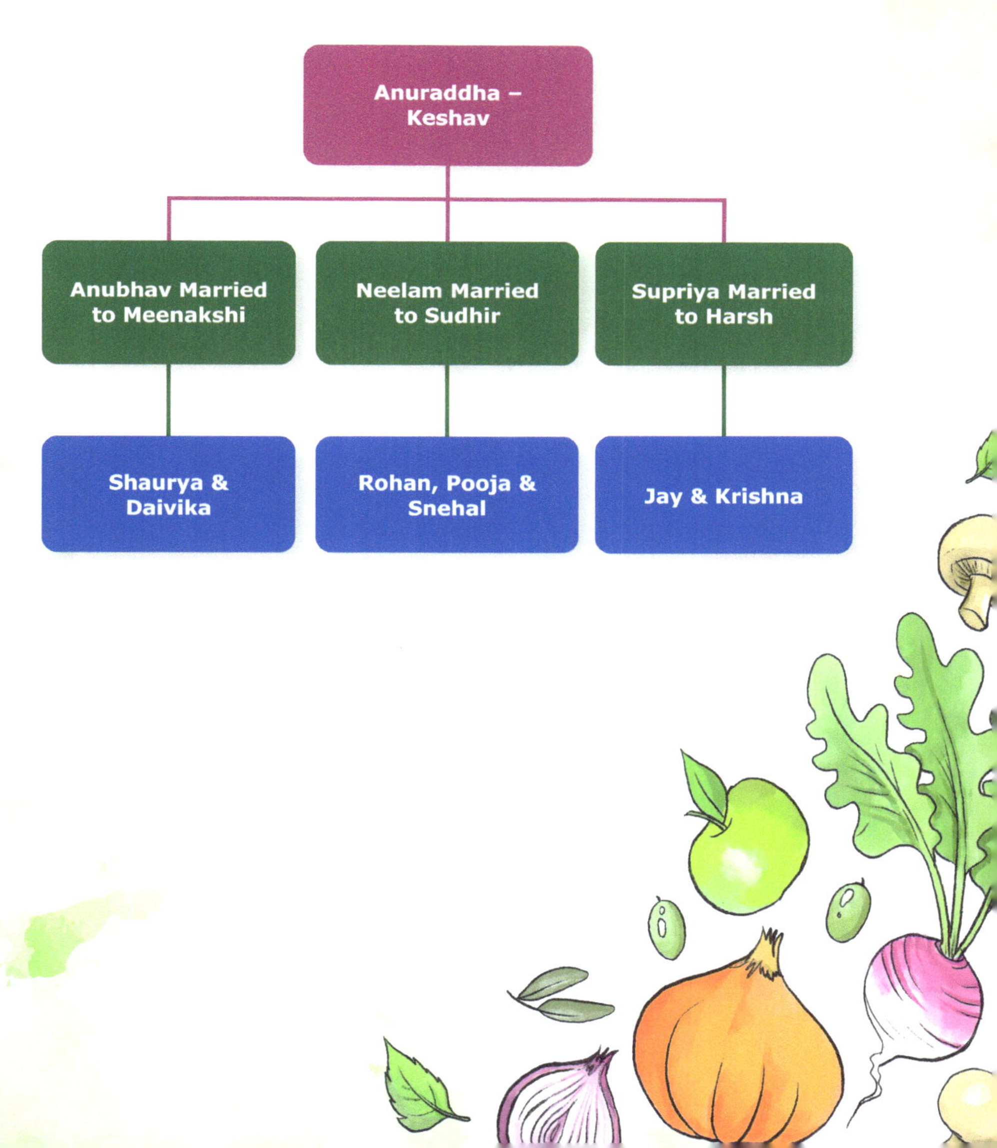

# Contents

# List of Recipes

Here are some simple recipes especially for children (but do take your parents or an elder's help when required)

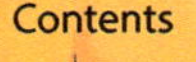

01

# How did it begin?

Krishna, a small girl, who loved cooking and experimenting all kinds of foodstuff in her kitchen. She was known as 'The Little Chef' in her school and was lovingly called Gopi at home

All loved whatever she cooked but she always wondered that why doesn't her food taste like that of her grandma's. One day as she was having snacks, she was thinking about her grandma's food and how it tasted better even though they both used the same recipe. She was in deep thoughts. Everybody was staring at her as to what was it that kept Krishna engaged. Krishna, The Lil' Chef loved cooking, but she also enjoyed talking to people; everybody was happy to see her blabber all the time but today they were surprised to see her so silent. Breaking the silence her mother, Supriya asked her "Krishna, why are you so distracted today dear? What are you thinking about?". Krishna was lost in thoughts of her own to notice her mother speak. Her mother tapped her hand and asked her several times. And finally, with a sudden jerk Krishna replied and said "Amma... can you tell me why doesn't my food taste like that of Ammama's". Krishna's mother laughed and said "My dear Gopi everyone has their own touch to the recipe although the recipe could

be the same. Maybe the time when the ingredients are put make a difference or maybe the salt, water, vegetables, and masala could be a little different. You would never know what brings this difference. Come here Gopi! There is another important ingredient that is added." "Yes, is it so? I don't know about it, Amma? Please tell me more about it!" "It is 'LOVE', the love and affection that ammama puts in while cooking all those yummy dishes you enjoy eating. Now this is what makes the recipes really different."

Krishna had a question mark on her face, Love? How is that possible amma, it's not an ingredient?

It's not a physical ingredient for sure but it is a sense that is only felt by the heart, it's not heard nor seen and not even tasted. Though Krishna's mother explained it to her, Krishna was too small and naive to understand what she meant. So, Krishna just nodded and walked off to the kitchen. Her mom knew she was young to understand this and she knew that Krishna had never felt that sense of love and warmth in the food that she made or ate. So, Supriya decided to send Krishna to her grandma's place so she could understand and experience these feelings herself.

Soon they started packing so that they could reach the airport as early as possible. While packing Jay, Krishna's younger brother said "Amma, I will feel lonely here please take me with you, here I don't even have any friends". Making a small puppy face he looked at his mother. She pulled his ears immediately and said "stop acting I know you want to eat all the delicious food that amma and Krishna will make, right? And don't lie to me you have more friends than one can ever have had in an entire life time, so stay here and enjoy your vacations with them and ajju-papama, we will be back just in a week's time or so."

Hearing all of these talks Krishna giggled and said "Let him come amma, at least I... I won't be bored, Supriya smiled and looked at them and thought in her mind. Both of you little children remind me of my childhood either you defend each other or fight like enemies forever. After hearing all of this noise papa came in and said "Everything's ready?" Both the children stood still because if they had fought like cats in front of papa he would start shouting and cancel all plans.

Papa suddenly laughed by looking at them because they stood straight like dolls and so he said "I don't shout at you for no reason children, it's just so that you don't get hurt" both the children got out of their 'SAVDHAAN' pose with a sigh of relief and began checking if they had taken everything before they left.

# The start of something new

The family had booked an early morning flight to go to Shirali in Karnataka where their ammama lived with ajju and a small little cat with her kittens in one old yet unique and beautiful bungalow. Krishna and Jay were excited to go to their native place, they loved their grandparents and loved to spend time learning new things from them. Supriya was also happy to see her parents after a long time, after all she missed them a lot. Soon the flight took off and Krishna waved her hand bidding goodbye to Mumbai for a few weeks.

By 10 o'clock all of them reached, their ammama was waiting at the gate of their mansion to welcome them with a plate decorated with flowers and bright Diya with some homemade sweets. She too looked forward to this small vacation with her adorable grandchildren and her daughter Supriya. Ajju was more excited to see them. He had arranged the bedrooms as the kids like it and prepared some welcome drink for them, using kokum and jaggery.

Krishna stepped into the house in astonishment seeing the arrangements made for her and decided to quickly have a bath. She didn't want to waste even a second so she came out in 2 minutes, all dressed up to

see what all was made at home. Jay on the other hand was lured to the kitchen by the aroma of freshly made sheera (type of sweet with semolina, sugar and ghee) by his Ammama. He was about to have it when Krishna saw that and stopped him saying "My dear brother, please go and wash your hands at once" with an angry and mature face. Supriya too shouted at him and said "Jay it is bad manners to sneak food like this, go have a bath first!!" Jay, with a frown, started walking towards the bathroom. Ammama couldn't see this frown so whispered to him and said "Pss, don't worry I promise no one will touch the sheera till you are out" and winked at him. His frown turned into a gentle smile and he walked towards the bathroom. Krishna pulled ammama down with a jerk and said "ammama can you quickly teach me something, something easy and quick to make."

Ammama nodded and said "Tell me what you want to learn? Which vegetable you want to use?" Immediately Krishna replied "TOMATOES! I remember ajju likes them so let's surprise him.

## Recipe 1

# Tomato Saar

*Tomato Saar is a tangy, soupy curry made with tomatoes coconut and Indian spices.*

### Ingredients:

- 6 Tomatoes
- 1 tbsp Freshly Grated Coconut
- 2 Green Chillies
- $\frac{1}{2}$ tsp Cumin Seeds
- $\frac{1}{4}$ Inch Piece Ginger
- $\frac{1}{2}$ tsp Mustard seeds
- 8 to 10 Curry leaves
- 1 Red Chilli {bedagi mirchi}
- 1 pinch of *Hing* {asafetida}

### Method:

- ☐ Rinse the tomatoes and put them in the boiling water for them to be blanched.
- ☐ Peel the skin and set it aside.

- ☐ Grind 1 tbsp of freshly grated coconut and add 2 chopped green chilies and half a teaspoon cumin seeds along with a small piece of ginger.
- ☐ Add the tomatoes to the dry mixture and grind it into a paste.
- ☐ Take a *kaylee* (deep bottomed pan) pour coconut oil in it and add half a teaspoon of mustard seeds and let them crackle for a while.
- ☐ Add $\frac{1}{4}$ teaspoon cumin seeds and let them crackle, then add 8 to 10 curry leaves, 1 broken red chili and a pinch of asafetida.
- ☐ Add the tomato puree to this tempering along with the remaining stock. Now cover the pan with a lid and allow the tempering flavors to get infused in the Saar for 3 to 4 minutes, you may also like adding coriander and sautéed onions if you wish to.
- ☐ Serve them in bowls and relish this easy and yummy dish.

"So did you enjoy making this preparation Gopi?" asked Ammama "Yes for sure I love the taste too. Let's give this to everyone!" All relished it, Jay was licking the bowl till he finished all of the Saar. Ammama and Krishna were happy seeing everyone enjoying the dish, after all what satisfies a chef is when they see full tummy's with a serene smile of satisfaction of having a dish made by their loved one.

# The Arrival of a Guest

After a lovely time in the morning the children, got a call from Neelam pacchi (aunty) she was Krishna's mother's (Supriya's) sister. She too had kids, three of them. Neelam pacchi had called to tell Ammama that she too was missing everyone after she saw those photos and messages on their WhatsApp group so was coming for a few weeks to live with all and have fun with everyone plus the kids wouldn't get bored when they play with each other.

Except Ammama, no one knew that they were coming but Krishna was curious so she was behind the door trying to listen to what Ammama was saying but all she could hear was 'the more the merrier'. Krishna was now happy because she knew someone was coming to stay with them.

She quickly ran to Jay's room and said "Quick Jay please help me" as she was picking pillows and blankets from the cabinet, "what happened?" asked Jay "I think someone is coming to stay with us!" whispered Krishna.

"WHAT?" shouted Jay "shhhshh......... I think it is Neelam Pacchi and our cousins" "Yay!!" again Jay shouted "Stop it! Jay, we have to make the preparations very quietly okay?".

By now Ammama was knowing that the children heard her conversation with Neelam, so she called everyone in the hall and told them that Neelam and kids were coming to stay with them for the summer vacation.

All got excited and ran to start making the arrangements, Supriya swept and mopped the floor, Ajju like always was decorating the rooms for the kids and Jay helped him with putting new lights. Ammama and Krishna went to the kitchen for making preparations. After all the preparations were done, they all gathered in the garden and picked some lovely flowers for the evening prayers. By the time the sun set, Neelam Pacchi and her 3 kids had reached. Their names were Snehal, she was as old as Krishna and loved to be with Krishna all the time. Rohan was the 2nd child he was 8 years old and loved video games, he hated cooking or being in the kitchen but loved having food. The 3rd and youngest one was Pooja, a 3-year-old cute child. All were excited to be there, they didn't interrupt in the prayers and quietly washed their hands and joined the prayer. Once it was done, all of them had a good chat till 8 in the evening. Now it was really late so Ammama told the four kids to have a wash and then come for food. While Neelam took Pooja to have a quick wash before her grandparents could pamper her with love. Everyone couldn't wait to taste what was made for dinner so they all finished bathing as soon as possible. All sat for dinner on the huge table and smelt the lovely aroma of the patravado along with hot masale bhaat and solkadi. Jay pulled the box of patravado and took 2 of them. Neelam and Supriya remembered their childhood when their mother used to make them succulent and crispy, just the way they liked it. Like always they asked their Amma for the recipe.

# Recipe 2

## Patravado

*Patravado is an authentic recipe made by Gujarati's, Maharashtrian's and very differently by the Konkani speaking communities who use ground chana dal for the masala. Here is an easy way to prepare it*

### Ingredients:

- 2 cups Besan
- $\frac{1}{4}$ cup Jaggery
- 1 tsp Turmeric
- 1 tsp Red chili powder
- 1 tsp Aamti powder
- Salt to taste
- 1 lemon size ball of Tamarind soaked in 3 tbsp of water to extract pulp
- Colocasia leaves

## Method:

- ☐ Prepare the besan mixture.
- ☐ Grate $\frac{1}{4}$ cup of Jaggery in a small bowl, in another bowl take 2 cups of besan, turmeric, red chili powder, *aamti* powder, salt and tamarind paste and all to taste. Now add the jaggery and mix till it has dissolved, you can also add oil and water to make it into a thick paste.
- ☐ Wash and remove the veins of the Colocasia leaves
- ☐ Apply the besan mixture on one leaf and place another leaf over it, make sure the mixture is evenly coated. Continue this method with other leaves.
- ☐ Roll up the leaves and steam for 20 mins
- ☐ Once cooled cut the rolls into half inch slices.
- ☐ (This is served with a coconut curry called *ghashhi)*, alternatively the slices may be roasted and tempered with mustard seeds, sesame seeds and asafoetida with a garnish of fresh coriander leaves.

### Recipe 3 & 4

# Masale Bhaat and Sol Kadi

## 03. Masale Bhaat:

*Flavored Maharashtrian rice preparation, a very quick recipe and mostly made for functions and for huge crowd of people.*

**Ingredients:**

- 1 cup rice
- 2 tbsps green peas
- Turmeric powder 1/2 tsp
- Aamti powder (special spice powder) 2 tsps
- Lavang (Cloves) 3 nos.
- Dalchini (Cinnamon) 1 inch
- Salt to taste
- Ghee 1 tbsp
- Broken kajus (cashews) 2 tbsps

## Method:

- ☐ Heat ghee in thick bottom pan.
- ☐ Add *lavang, dalchini* and *kaju* and roast slightly.
- ☐ Add the washed rice turmeric and *aamti* powder.
- ☐ Boil 2 cups of water with salt and peas.
- ☐ On boiling add to rice.
- ☐ Cover the lid and allow to simmer and cook.
- ☐ Garnish with freshly grated coconut, a dash of lime and finely chopped coriander leaves.

And the yummy rice dish is hot and ready to savor!!

## 04. Solkadi

*A typical Konkani beverage. Slightly pungent and sour, it is an effective appetizer.*

### *Ingredients:*

- 1 cup of freshly grated coconut
- 2 tbsp dried Kokum
- Garlic flakes 4 cloves
- 1 green chilly

### *Method:*

- ☐ Grind all ingredients into a fine paste.
- ☐ Strain well through a strainer.
- ☐ Add salt to taste.
- ☐ And the cooling drink is ready, to go well with the spicy rice masale bhaat!!

# When Love Starts with Hate

Lovely Amma, said both the sisters, they loved all the food that was made and the children too were very happy. All of them started appreciating ammama Ammama a lot. Krishna was slightly jealous; this was the first time Krishna felt envious about something and she knew that it is not right. She knew that one should not feel jealousy towards anybody's success rather should cheer for them and learn from their victory. Though all didn't realize this only Ammama understood and knew what is going on in this tiny little mind. So, she gathered everybody and told them a short story of her childhood. Ammama also loved telling stories like every other grandma.

Anuradha who is now a grandma to these seven children was once a small girl too. She loved cooking just like Krishna but her father never openly acknowledged that he was proud of her. And that is what Anuradha hated, but she also challenged him and tried all kinds of recipes to impress him but nothing seemed to work.

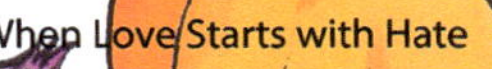

One day her father's friend's son who also loved cooking came to their house as a guest. While he was there, he made some excellent motichoor ladoos for them. Anuradha's father praised that boy so much that it made her feel jealous of him and for many days she hated him and avoided speaking to him. However, as they started spending time with each other, they became friends and soon they were tied in the beautiful knot of marriage - the purest form of a romantic relation in this world, a relation which is full of love and respect for each other.,. Today that boy too has become a grandfather and his name is Keshav!

All of them were pleasantly surprised because Keshav was their grandfather. No one knew about this story till date except Keshav and Anuradha themselves. Krishna was awestruck she completely forgot the fact that she was jealous about 10 mins ago and was so lost in the story that she said "Hence this relation today will be given a quote which says 'when love starts with hate'", and today I know why this is a match made in heaven cause Anuradha is another name to goddess

Radha and Keshav is another name of Lord Shri Krishn" added Supriya.

Okay! Then, let's make a quick recipe that always reminds me of them.

## Recipe 5

# Rice Kheer

*Rice kheer a specialty when it comes to RadhaKrishn, it was known that both enjoyed this dish and relished it when they had it together. To know how to make some, please do check the recipe*

### Ingredients:

- 1 litre milk
- $\frac{1}{4}$ cup sugar
- $\frac{1}{4}$ cup-soaked rice (soaked for approximately 20 to 30 mins)
- 1 tsp cardamom powder
- 7 to 8 saffron strands soaked in 2 tbsp milk
- 2 tsp of chopped dry fruits for garnish.

### Method:

- ☐ Take a vessel let it heat for a while and then pour the milk in it. Keep stirring for a while
- ☐ Now add the rice once the milk has come to a little boil and cook the rice for about 10 minutes

- ☐ Once the rice has cooked add the sugar in the vessel
- ☐ Then add the saffron and mix it well till the sugar dissolves.
- ☐ Once dissolved add the cardamom powder and stir well.
- ☐ After sometime add the dry fruits.
- ☐ Serve it in a bowl and garnish with some more dry fruits you can also place a tulsi (Basil) leaf if you wish to, and here it is ready in front of you. I hope you feel blissful after you have had this.

"So, did all of you enjoy making this?" asked Ammama. "Surely, I enjoyed it a lot and perhaps it's been long since I have made food with everyone together where we all give our contribution in making something," said Snehal. "Yes, I believe we all love a little company, it makes everything so much more fun," said Supriya.

# A Nostalgic Moment

Now it was the next day, and it was almost dusk time. All children had finished playing in the veranda and Ajju had finished feeding some milk and biscuits to the cats and its kittens. Supriya and Neelam were making some tea for everyone and were talking to each other about how life had been lately. They remembered all of their childhood days when they were so connected with each other. Now they had drifted apart for so many years that they couldn't even take out time to speak to each other and were not in close contact for really long. They both were very happy to see that after so many days they got the time to sit and chat. Their chat went on for long a time, in fact it took so long that Ammama had to call them for the evening prayers.

After the prayers were recited, everyone went back to do their work. Ammama went into the kitchen to see what was to be made for dinner, Krishna followed her. Snehal was checking if any home work was remaining so that she could finish it then itself. Jay and Rohan were playing Chess and Ajju was pacifying Pooja by making her laugh. But Supriya and Neelam were still talking. Looking at this Ammama whispered in Krishna's ears "Let's surprise them. Come I will teach you how to make one dish that both of these 'little' sisters enjoyed having when they were as old as you" "Yay!!" Krishna said in a low voice "A recipe that amma likes? This is so exciting!"

## Recipe 6, 7 & 8

# Appe and Chutney & Besan Ladoos

### 6. Appe:

*Appe can be called as roasted or shallow fried dumplings. They are bite size, fluffy and light also very soft on the inside and crispy on the outside when we talk about their texture. Mostly made in South-Indian homes as a breakfast dish or even relished during snack time.*

***Ingredients:***

- $2^1/_2$ cups Urad dal
- 1 cup (Semolina)
- Salt to taste
- Oil to fry

## Method:

- ☐ White Urad Dal soak 21/2 cups over-night.
- ☐ Grind to a fine batter
- ☐ Add 1 cup rava
- ☐ Add salt to taste
- ☐ Take an appe pan
- ☐ Heat well apply oil to the surface of all the concaves.
- ☐ Gently pour the batter into the cups.
- ☐ Cover with a lid.
- ☐ Allow to roast on a slow flame for crispy well-cooked appe.
- ☐ After sometime gently cook on other side too.

## 7. Chutney

*Tangy spice dip special had with appe*

### Ingredients:

- Quarter tsp *urad dal*
- 2 red dried chilies [*Bedagi mirchi*]
- 1 cup coconut [freshly grated]
- And a little tamarind
- Curry leaves
- Mustard seeds
- *Hing* [asafetida]
- 1 tsp Coconut oil

### Method:

- ☐ Roast the *urad dal* and red chilies.
- ☐ After that grind it with freshly grated coconut along with tamarind and salt into a smooth thick paste.
- ☐ Temper it with mustard seeds, *hing* and curry leaves with coconut oil.

## *8. Besan Ladoos*

*A perfect Indian delicacy for a person with a sweet tooth*

### *Ingredients:*

- *1 cup Besan*
- *$\frac{1}{2}$ cup Ghee*
- *Handful of Kismis* (Dried grapes)
- One pinch of Cardamom powder
- 1 cup Powdered sugar

- ☐ Roast 2 cups of besan in a thick bottom pan along with one cup pure ghee.
- ☐ Roast it thoroughly on a slow flame till the besan turns golden yellow with a strong aroma of roasted besan.
- ☐ Switch off the flame.

- ☐ Add a handful of *kismis* and 2 pinches of cardamom powder.
- ☐ Add the powdered sugar, mold into small *ladoos*.
- ☐ One *kismis* per *ladoo* can be squeezed to add a tempting appeal.

# A Night Out in the Veranda

"Thank you so much Amma and Krishna", both the sisters said in sync. Krishna and Ammama smiled at them. Now it was time to sleep. All the children started fighting about who will sleep with Ammama and Ajju, Ajju told them not to scream and suddenly the electricity went off. Now what is to be done! Said Rohan. "Now all of us will sleep in the veranda" said ammama, Yay!!! All screamed with joy.

Actually, this all was a plan made by Snehal and Jay. They knew that all will want to sleep with Ammama and so they decided to turn off the electricity switches and then all could sleep in the garden. Everyone quickly brought out the bed sheets, mattress, 2 mosquito nets and 3 packs of cards.

Everybody began neatly assembling their beds and making other arrangements but Snehal and Jay were trying to get the garden lights on, thankfully the garden lights had some other switch too. So, they all started playing cards and singing songs from the films they had watched earlier. Soon as they were giggling and recalling their funny childhood stories till they all fell asleep.

Now it was 6 o'clock in the morning Ammama started with her morning chores of having bath, making breakfast, and singing bhajans to gain peace of mind. Today there was lovely *Upma* made for breakfast, the aroma of the *Upma* had woken up both the boys. To their astonishment Krishna had made today's breakfast. Besides Upma, she had also made hot tea and sabudana vada.

## Recipe 8 & 9

# Sabudana vadas and Upma

## 08. Sabudana Vada:

*Sabudana Vada is a Fried Lip-smacking snack. It has a crispy layer on the outside and is soft and flavorful on the inside. It is generally served with sweetened curd.*

### Ingredients:

- 2 cups Sabudana (Sago)
- 4 potatoes small boiled
- 2 tsp Jeera (Cumin seeds)
- $\frac{1}{4}$ tsp of Hing (asafetida)
- 6 finely chopped green chilies
- Finely chopped coriander
- {Haldi (turmeric) Red chili powder} optional

## Method:

- ☐ Wash and soak the sabudana over night.
- ☐ Boil the potatoes, peel, and mash them along with the green chillies, Hing and jeera.
- ☐ Add finely chopped coriander leaves.
- ☐ Mix the sabudana with the mixture thoroughly.
- ☐ Shape into small flattened vadas.
- ☐ Deep fry until golden brown on medium frame.

## 09. Upma

*Soft, warm and soothing breakfast item also preferred during fasting. Easy and quick to prepare.*

### Ingredients:

- *Rava* 1 cup (Semolina)
- *Ghee* 1 tbsp
- For tempering ½ tsp Mustard seeds
- ¼ tsp *Urad Dal*
- 2 Green chilies
- One sprig of Curry leaves
- Coriander finely chopped
- Salt and Sugar to taste

### Method:

- ☐ Lightly roast the *rava* in *ghee.*
- ☐ Set aside, meanwhile 3 cups of water with the required salt and sugar to be kept for boiling.
- ☐ In a *kadhai* (frying pan) take some ghee or oil, on heating add all the ingredients for tempering. Let the mustard seeds splutter well.
- ☐ To this let the *rava* and water be added.
- ☐ Step 5: Cover with a lid and allow to flavors to mix till the *rava* is cooked.
- ☐ Step 6: Serve hot with coriander garnish and a dash of lemon along with *shev* or mix *farsan.*

# The Opposite Ends

Now it was noon all the children had finished bathing and were sitting and doing their homework. Suddenly they heard someone screaming "hello papama see who has come," the voice was very familiar, to know who it is, all the children left whatever they were doing and saw that it was Abhinav mamu with Meenakshi mami and their 2 kids Shaurya and Daivika. They too had come to stay with them this summer. All were very happy because they lived in the U.S. and after many years they had come back to India.

Krishna loved to spend time with Daivika because both had similar interest and had lots to share, for example Daivika loved gardening and growing different vegetables and Krishna used to use those vegetables to make healthy food dishes. They both chit-chatted and did everything together. Snehal too was very happy, as she too was as old as them and was a part of the trio.

The 3 sisters were like best friends Daivika used to teach them how to plant, Snehal used to tell the medicinal value or the nutrients in it and Krishna used to cook all types of dishes with those vegetables. But the boys on the other hand were complete opposites, Rohan used to teach how to play the video game, Shaurya used to tell what are the myths and rumors he searched about the game online and Jay used to experiment all the different games. All the seven children were very different except one thing; they did have something in common which was mangoes all of them loved mangoes more than anything else in this world obviously even Pooja used to enjoy it.

So, on that note Krishna told everyone that she will make a special mango dish this year.

# Recipe 10

# Mango Kulfi

*A Mango Kulfi recipe that is quick, easy and a cheat's version made with milk, sweetened condensed milk, cream and sweet tasting mangoes. Make this super simple summer treat and cherish with your special ones*

## Ingredients:

- 1.5 cup milk
- 200ml Condensed milk
- 1.5 cup Cream
- Cardamom powder
- Crushed Saffron
- Kulfi molds or bowls

## Method:

- ☐ Add 1.5 cups whole milk, sweetened condensed milk (200 grams or 200 ml) and 1 cup chopped mangoes in a blender jar.

**TIP:** You can use an immersion blender as well to make the mango kulfi mixture.

- ☐ Blend everything until smooth.
- ☐ Then add $\frac{1}{2}$ cup cream. You can include light cream, heavy cream or whipping cream.
- ☐ Sprinkle the cardamom powder and crushed saffron. Blend again until the cream is mixed well.

**TIP:** Do a taste test and add 1 to 2 tablespoons of sweetened condensed milk if you find the sweetness to be less.

- ☐ If the sweetness is more for your liking, add 1 to 2 tablespoons of cream. Give a quick blitz again in the blender.
- ☐ Pour the kulfi mixture in kulfi moulds or small bowls. Cover tightly with a lid or seal with aluminium foil and keep in the freezer for 6 to 8 hours for the kulfi to set.
- ☐ To remove the kulfi, place the moulds under running water for some seconds or rub them between your palms. With a butter knife, gently remove the kulfi. Then slice it on a chopping board.

- ☐ Serve mango kulfi slices in bowls or plates, sprinkled with cardamom powder or crushed saffron.
- ☐ It can also be paired with cooked falooda sev (thin vermicelli) and soaked sabja seeds (Chia Seeds). You can also add some rose syrup on the mango kulfi slices while serving.

08

# A Lesson for Rohan

"That was lip-smacking Krishna, just speechless" said Daivika "So now that we all have learnt something new can we move on and can you all please help me, Supriya and amma in making papads? " added Neelam, "okay" said all of the kids with a little frown on their faces.

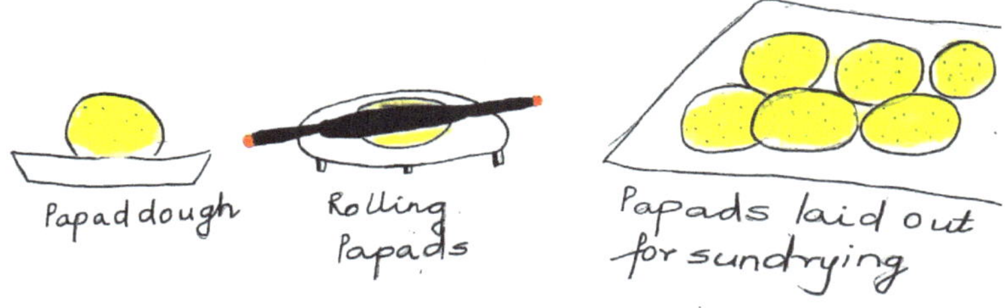


Now all started helping, first in making the dough then kneading it properly, after that they went in the gallery to make papads and then dry them. In this activity all were equally taking part except Rohan he was continuously saying "I will come in a minute" Neelam felt very embarrassed so she was repeatedly telling him to come right away but he didn't pay any heed. Everyone was busy doing something or the other so no one really noticed except Ammama. She told Neelam not to worry as he was just a child and that he will understand the meaning of spending quality time with family after this short story. "Come on everyone let the papads dry now. I will tell you something exciting" said Ammama to all of them. "What is it Papama why have you called us?" asked Shaurya with curiosity, "I have called you to tell you a story", "Yay story time!!" shouted the children.

Once upon a time there lived a young youth named Ram who lived in the village of Gokul, He had got married at a young age of 20. His wife's name was Vaidehi. She was a beautiful and really hardworking woman, whereas her husband, Ram was a lazy man. He never helped her in any work and because he wasn't earning any money, she had to start farming all by herself. Just after 3 months of their marriage Ram's elder brother named Prathamesh who had a big business and a small family with his wife and two children, came across a big loss in his business, he lost a lot of the things- his three plots, one big mansion and a lot of money. He didn't have a house to stay so he asked Vaidehi if she knew anyone who has a house where he could live. She suggested that they can live in her and Ram's house till his business is back on track. So just the next week Prathamesh and his family came to Ram's house. Ram wasn't bothered that his brother has visited his place, he just slept all day long. His brother used to get angry on him that now he is married he has to look after another person too. But Ram wouldn't listen to a single word. It was like speaking to a deaf man. Gradually a month passed by, Prathamesh still needed some more money to buy another house. All of them used to make food together and Prathamesh used to look into his business matters. On weekends he too would do some small house hold chores. They all enjoyed doing those jobs, they did everything together excepting Ram who always gave excuses to not get up and work. Though he slept all the time he observed how quickly work used to get over. Soon Prathamesh and his wife had to leave because they found a decent house to live in and managed to get things back on track. Vaidehi felt really bad because she got used to them being around and within two days she too had to go to her mother's place for few weeks. Vaidehi's father wasn't keeping well. So, Ram couldn't stop her.

Now Ram had to sit at home alone and had to do the chores himself. Vaidehi knew this was the best time to teach him a lesson so before leaving when he was asleep, she just made the house a little dirty, to see whether he will clean it or no. For many days

Ram didn't do anything and the house became worse than what it was. Around this time there was a terrible disease that had taken over the village and the doctors there predicted that the main reason behind it is dust and that's why advised all to clean their houses regularly. People weren't listening and it became very contagious so the police in the village decided to start taking rounds and check each house just for the villagers' safety. When Ram heard this, he was shocked because every nook and corner of his house was full of dust and dirt. So, he decided to clean. He didn't know what to do because he had never done it and started crying because he remembered that things happened so fast and with so much ease when all worked together and now when he had to do it alone, he had no one to help he begged to his wife to come back home and help him.

After that day he realized what a great mistake he had done by not helping his wife and then he found a good job which paid him enough for his wife and himself. Soon they too had a baby girl and they lived happily ever after.

"So, Rohan dear what did you understand from this story", Rohan looked down with embarrassment and said "Yes, I am sorry to all that I didn't help you all while making the papads but now while roasting them I will surely be in the kitchen and roast one per head and 5 for me." All of them laughed together.

# Many Months Later...

Now the month of May had gone past, in fact even the half of the monsoons were over. Still the lockdown isn't opened so the day of going back home was just postponing, the children's fathers used to come and stay for once in a while but then had to leave soon because offices had slowly started opening up.

Now the month of August had started. It is almost the last week. Everyone is very excited, for what you may ask? It's Raksha Bandhan this weekend. A day on which the relation of a brother and sister is celebrated. One of the most beautiful relationships. This relation has many flavors, sometimes it's sweet, or bitter, sometimes it can be spicy and sour too, isn't it a relation with every flavor? It definitely is. Let's see what the siblings of the Naik family are planning for this year's Raksha Bandhan.

"Yay! Sunday is Raksha Bandhan" Krishna jumped with glee and danced round the drawing room. "Oh yes" said Snehal, and on the other hand little Pooja smiled and laughed with a twinkle in her eye. "Oh yeah the day when I am supposed to protect Supriya, my ***small little*** sister" said Abhinav in a sarcastic way. "Not only today Abhinav dada", said Neelam "it is a brother's responsibility to always take care of his sister because we have a blood relation and that's why it is your responsibility" ……. "But I don't agree with you" said Ammama. All looked at her with astonishment that why is Ammama saying that. "Papama!!? What are you saying isn't this festival all about how a brother must always try his best to keep his sisters safe and happy?" added Daivika. "Yes, truly this festival is about a brother's promise to his sister for her happiness and safety, but do you children know the story of this festival?" asked Ammama. "Not really Ammama……… I do remember few parts of it because it was told few years back in school, but would love listening to it again and this time will remember the story.

"Okay then, I think I must tell you all this lovely story right after we are done cooking today's lunch and also the reason why I didn't agree with Neelam".

"Ammama, today only we kids will make something and you will taste it okay?"

## Recipe 11

# Kaju Katli

*A popular Indian sweet dessert recipe made with powdered cashew and sugar syrup. It is perhaps one of the popular Indian sweet recipes which are made for all celebrations, occasions, and festival seasons.*

### Ingredients:

- You'll need **3 main ingredients (cashews, sugar and water).**

### Method:

- ☐ First, remove the required number of cashews from the fridge and **let cashews come to room temperature**. It may take 1-2 hours. This is an important step and you cannot skip it.
- ☐ Take that into a food processor and make powder by using the pulse button. **Do not over-grind** otherwise, it starts to release the oil and becomes wet, pasty. We need dry powder here.
- ☐ Take sugar and water in a heavy bottom pan on medium-low heat.

- ☐ Let it just come to a boil (no need to simmer).
- ☐ As soon as it starts boiling add cashew powder.
- ☐ And mix it and cook with stirring constantly.
- ☐ As it gets cooked, it starts to get thick and leaves the sides of the pan. Do not scrap the thin layer that stuck to the pan as it has become chewy now.
- ☐ Keep cooking until it comes together like a dough. Depending on the gas heat and size/shape of the pan, it may take around 8-10 minutes.
- ☐ ***CHECK:*** *Take a small portion, blow it so it is touchable, make a small ball and if it is sticking to the finger it needs more cooking. If not sticking then it is ready.*
- ☐ Remove it to a greased plate and let it cool to touch. **It should be warm (not cooled completely).**
- ☐ Once it is cool to handle, grease your hand with ghee and knead it two-three times.
- ☐ Make a smooth dough. **DO NOT over-knead it.**
- ☐ Now take a big piece of parchment paper. Put the dough ball on it and using your hand start patting and make a thick round patty. So now it will be easier to roll.
- ☐ Cover the dough with another piece of parchment paper and start rolling. The thickness should be ¼ inch to ⅓ inch. Do not roll it too thin. The circle was approx. 10-12 inches in diameter.

IMPORTANT NOTE: do the kneading and rolling job while the dough is still warm. If it gets cool, it will start to set and becomes hard to roll.

- ☐ Using a knife cut into a diamond shape. Now let it cool completely and set. It may take around 15 minutes.
- ☐ Now apply the silver leaf on kaju katli. This is optional but it looks good and just like the store-bought kind. Working with varak is very tricky, you should be very careful and do not touch it with your hand.

*Wow that was amazing, children! And as promised now I will tell all of you the beautiful story of Raksha Bandhan.*

"Now kids there are many stories in which people believe in. It is said that because that particular phenomenon occurred, we celebrate Raksha Bandhan. I too know many such stories but I think I will tell you the most famous one and my favorite too.

"So, children do you know the story of The Epic Mahabharata". "Yes, we do!!" all said in sync. "Okay then let me start with this lovely story."

## Krishna and Draupadi - The Unending Book

This is a mythological story and a very interesting one. The story is about Raksha Bandhan and is specially narrated to children, so that they know the importance of this day and the bond of a brother and sister. This story is from the grand epic Mahabharata.

Princess Draupadi was the wife of the five Pandavas. Krishna was their friend and mentor. Draupadi respected Krishna a lot. She used to call him 'Sakha' which means a friend who is like a sibling to you and always held him in high regard.

One day in the court, Krishna faced a difficult situation. His Bua's son Shishupal was threatening to kill him! Shishupal and Krishna had always had a strained relationship. This went back to the time when Shishupal was born with three eyes and four arms. When his parents pleaded to the heavens, a voice told them - "The one in whose lap Shishupal's extra arms and eye will disappear will also be his killer." This turned out to be Krishna, who was still a child at that time. Upon seeing his bua's horror, he told her, "Please don't worry. I promise you I will forgive 100 mistakes made by Shishupal."

However, today, Shishupal was seething in anger. Krishna had married the princess Rukmini - a princess Shishupal himself had wanted to marry and also what raged Shishupal's anger was that even after getting married to princess Rukmini, he loved and always wanted Radha to be with him. In his anger, when he surpassed even 100 fits of abuse, Krishna could not take it anymore. He flung his Sudarshan Chakra at Shishupal and killed him. However, while doing so, Krishna also hurt his finger because the Chakra was on his finger for a long time till Shishupal went pleading to all the people in the court.

Draupadi was watching all this, even Radha was able to see this with the help of her inner eyes. Radha immediately told Draupadi to tie a piece of cloth on Krishna's finger. Unable to bear the sight of Krishna's blood, she hastily tore off a part of her sari. Using this cloth, she bandaged his finger and stopped the blood flow. Krishna was extremely touched by her gesture. He promised to protect her whenever she needed him, whenever she was in distress. To bless her, he uttered the word 'Akshyam'. It means - 'May it be unending'.

Years later, the Pandavas were facing a major defeat and humiliation at the hands of their brothers, the Kauravas. They had lost in a game of dice, and as per the 'rule', lost everything they owned - including their kingdom, and Draupadi. She was called to court, and the evil Dushasana tried to disrobe her. But no matter how hard he tried, he could not do it. The sari never seemed to end, and Draupadi's honour was intact. She was saved from facing embarrassment in the court.

And that is why on this auspicious day of Raksha Bandhan we celebrate the beautiful relation and the bond between a brother and a sister.

So, children did you all enjoy this lovely story of Raksha Bandhan? "YES" all of the children screamed on the top of their voice. "But Ammama why do you disagree with Amma asked Snehal. "Oh yes, I totally forgot about that. So, the reason why I disagreed with her was because I wanted to tell all of you that, even if the person is not your brother by a blood relation what matters is whether you accept him as a brother. "Uhhh!, Papama I didn't really understand what you wanted to conclude," said Shauray. "Okay let me explain, now if you see everyone says that your school is your second home yes, or no? "Yes Ammama, Rohan always says that," said Jay. "Yes, so now you tell me what does he actually mean". "I have never really thought of it," said Jay. "Okay then I will tell you what he means, Rohan says this because you are supposed to treat your friends and teachers like your family, surely there should be a distance and some respect as a student towards your teachers but you must treat your friends like how you treat a brother or a sister of yours, now did you get me?" asked Ammama. "Yes, now we know what you meant". And most importantly a fact that many people till date don't understand is that the 'Rakhi' or the thread is not only tied by a sister to her brother for her protection but also for his protection, it signifies that both the siblings should always be able to stand for each other in tough times.

# A Dawn of Enlightenment

## Recipe 12

# Vanilla Chocolate Chip Cupcakes

*Soft and delicious sweet little cupcakes for the ones with a sweet tooth*

### *Ingredients:*

- 1 cup Maida
- $\frac{3}{4}$ cup Sugar Powder
- $\frac{1}{2}$ tsp Baking Powder
- $\frac{1}{4}$ tsp Baking Soda
- Pinch of salt
- $\frac{1}{2}$ cup Butter/Oil
- $\frac{3}{4}$ cup Milk
- 2 tsp Vinegar
- $\frac{1}{2}$ cup Milk powder
- 2 tsp Vanilla essence

### *Method:*

- ☐ Sieve Maida, Baking powder, baking soda, salt, and keep it aside.
- ☐ Mix the milk and vinegar and set that aside for about 2 mins.

- ☐ After milk cuddles add oil, vanilla, sugar, milk powder and mix well with whipping machine.
- ☐ Next add all the dry ingredients part by part.
- ☐ Mix with a whipping machine for a minute
- ☐ Fill the mixture in moulds (3/4$^{th}$ portion)
- ☐ Sprinkle Choco chips/ nuts on top
- ☐ Bake at 180 degrees Celsius, for 18 to 20 mins

It was the next day after Raksha Bandhan. Raghu kaka their delivery boy who always sent them groceries by now had become great friends with the children and loved spending time with them, after all he knew their family for almost two decades.

So just the next day after the lovely celebration of the festival he had come to deliver some stuff and also decided to talk to the children for a while. All the children pulled him to the hall and asked him to sit down, soon they got two plates in front of him filled with delicious and mouth-watering cupcakes. Jay said, "Kaka, one of theseAmmama has made and the other one was made by Krishna. So, we want you to guess just by tasting who has made which of these, if you lose you have to take us to the fair in the evening." He thought for a while and then he said "okay, challenge accepted." Then he tasted one of them and he said, "I am a little confused can anyone of you help me to make a guess? Maybe someone who doesn't know who has made which one." "Sure, Kaka I can help." Said Jay. He came and tasted both of them. Within no time he looked at Krishna and whispered in her ears, "You made these ones, right?" Krishna stood aghast, even though the cupcakes tasted the same and the same recipe and ingredients, and even when Jay didn't know about who has made which slot, how could he tell it so confidently that I have made these..............................

And I guess, that's why my friend's love too is an ingredient.

Thank you!!

# Glossary

Amma - Mother

Ammama - Maternal Grandmother

Masala - Masala is loosely translated as "spice" and although there are many varieties and preferences masalas are typically made up of 5 spices. Cardamom, cinnamon, coriander, cloves, and cumin are mixed to make an aromatic and flavour profile.

Savdhaan - The caution position

Shirali - Shirali is a village in Bhatkal taluk of Uttara Kannada district in Karnataka. Shirali is home to two prominent temples: the Chitrapur Math and the Maha Ganapathi Mahammaya Temple. The Chitrapur Math is the holiest temple of the Chitrapur Saraswat Brahmin community, and the Maha Ganapathi Mahammaya temple is the Kuladev to the Kamaths, Bhats, Puraniks, Prabhus,

Joishys, Mallyas, Kudvas and Nayak families from the Goud Saraswat Brahmin community.

Ajju - It is referred to both paternal and maternal grandfather.

Sheera - Type of sweet dish made with semolina sugar and ghee

Pacchi - Maternal aunt

Papama - Paternal Grandmother

Mamu - Maternal uncle

Mami - Maternal uncle's wife

Bua - Paternal aunt

Pandavas - Since Pandu could not continue to remain the king of Hastinapur due to a curse given by his brother Dhritirashtra, his cousin-brother was made the king and Pandu's five sons chose to be called Pandava

Kauravas - The name Kaurava comes from the lineage of Dhritirashtra's ancestor Kuru, a dynamic king and ruler of the earth to all its corners, hence the heirs of the Kuru lineage termed as Kaurava.

www.ingramcontent.com/pod-product-compliance
Lightning Source LLC
LaVergne TN
LVHW021259160826
845679LV00001B/133

* 9 7 9 8 8 9 6 1 0 6 6 2 3 *